Weather
Fog

by Brienna Rossiter

FOCUS
READERS

SCOUT

www.focusreaders.com

Focus Readers is distributed by North Star Editions: sales@northstareditions.com | 888-417-0195

Produced for Focus Readers by Red Line Editorial.

Photographs ©: Lenka_N/Shutterstock Images, cover, 1; Amonthep Inseesungwon/ Shutterstock Images, 4 (top), 16 (top left); Alexander Kockin/Shutterstock Images, 4 (bottom); Piotr Krzeslak/Shutterstock Images, 7; Efimenko Alexander/Shutterstock Images, 9; vladimir salman/Shutterstock Images, 11; Matt Gibson/Shutterstock Images, 13, 16 (bottom right); daniilphotos/Shutterstock Images, 15, 16 (top right); kzww/Shutterstock Images, 16 (bottom left)

Library of Congress Cataloging-in-Publication Data
Names: Rossiter, Brienna, author.
Title: Fog / by Brienna Rossiter.
Description: Lake Elmo, MN : Focus Readers, [2020] | Series: Weather | Audience: K to grade 3. | Includes index.
Identifiers: LCCN 2018051344 (print) | LCCN 2018052059 (ebook) | ISBN 9781644930069 (pdf) | ISBN 9781641859271 (ebook) | ISBN 9781641857895 (hardcover) | ISBN 9781641858588 (pbk.)
Subjects: LCSH: Fog--Juvenile literature.
Classification: LCC QC929.F7 (ebook) | LCC QC929.F7 R67 2020 (print) | DDC 551.57/5--dc23
LC record available at https://lccn.loc.gov/2018051344

Printed in the United States of America
Mankato, MN
May, 2019

About the Author

Brienna Rossiter is a writer and editor who lives in Minnesota. She loves learning random facts by reading books, going to museums, and traveling to new places.

What Is Fog?

Fog looks like a **cloud**.

But it stays low.

It is near the ground.

Water **drops** make fog.

The drops are tiny.

They hang in the air.

How Fog Forms

We see fog on cool days.

Air moves over cold ground.

The air cools.

Air has water in it.

The water cools, too.

Drops form.

Fog appears.

Kinds of Fog

Some fog is thick.

It is wet.

It hides **trees**.

People cannot see far.

Some fog is thin.

Thin fog is called **mist**.

mist

Glossary

cloud

mist

drops

trees

Index